I DARE YOU TO WIN

THIS TIME YOU WIN

KANITA WASHINGTON

Kanita Washington (signature)

Edited by
NICOLE QUEEN

For every person who desires a big win at life...

CONTENTS

PREFACE

Moments between yesterday and today are filled with memories we love and regrets we wish to forget. Have you ever wished you could turn back the hands of time and relive your past? Perhaps you'd like to relive seeing a newborn baby being born or experiencing the joy of two hearts joining as one on a whimsical wedding day! Or, maybe you remembered that moment when you earned a promotion at work or when you realized you were at the pinnacle of your game. What if your treasured moment was the time when you wished you'd said, "I love you!" before someone special died— or even a golden opportunity that passed by, leaving you with regrets and grief.

Friend, I sympathize with your joy and pain. I know that these and other unforgettable, impressionable moments may have altered the course of your life forever. But what if God gave you the opportunity to relive just one moment from your past— would you? Which moment would you choose? Perhaps, you'd love to wipe off an unspeakable mistake from your past or savor a magical moment. What would you do if you had the power and ability to go back in time?

It is clear to the wise and seasoned that there is no reverse gear on the train of life! Knowing that the past is gone may be saddening, but is good news because it signals that the future is coming. And although this moment is a gift, we cannot hold on to it.

But here's the good news! Even though it's impossible to travel back in time, God has engineered a better future for us. This means that there's no need to despair because we cannot alter the past; therefore, we must remain hopeful because God has our future in His Hands. The good news is that God has shared His divine, creative power with us. He has made us co-creators and co-heirs with Him. He has blessed us with creativity and our desire should always be to please Him. Therefore, when we are aligned with His will, we can utilize His power to walk out the life He desires for us to live. Yet, with great power comes great responsibility to produce!

In what ways can you alter your narrative and position yourself for results on a different level? Do you know the power you possess? Or, do you feel that success is a function of time or an outcome of principles?

It's no wonder, with so many inquiries that may frequently run through our minds, it can be a daily struggle to stay afloat! Amidst so many life stressors, do you find it difficult to wait? Do you feel like something is missing? Do you sometimes crave that "aha" moment where everything clicks in place? Having to wait can be frustrating, as time endlessly passes by.

Have you ever asked yourself, "When will it ever be my time to win?" Are you tired of watching things happen around you, but feeling left out? Is your life spinning out of control, as you desperately feel like you could use a break? Each day may present a new challenge along the journey to victory, as your final resolution remains to win!

Does it seem that you are far away from winning? Or, can you taste how close you are to victory? Many of us have felt like we're in a downward spiral. But what if you could stop that downward spiral where everything that could possibly go wrong no longer goes wrong?

If any of the aforementioned experiences reflect your current situation, then you're holding the right book. Also know that you are not alone. Life was the same for me until something major happened— and the discourse of my life changed forever.

My moment happened when I was a contestant on *The Price is Right*, a very popular daytime television game show. I learned so much on this day, and my life was changed forever. There were so many circumstances stacked against me, while other factors worked in my favor behind the scenes.

This season taught me a powerful lesson: life can be a bittersweet experience. All of life's bright spots and dark undertones come together into one big package called life. But your ability to exercise principles that amplify its goodness and manage its challenges will make you come out on top every time.

This book was written to help you to understand the importance of taking the good with the bad, seeing the positive side of everything, and becoming in tune with your inner voice so that you can unlock the winner within. And as a result of my experience, I've honed seven principles that modified my life forever.

The words on these pages are gemstones for you to add to your treasure box of life lessons. Our discussion will be centered around the seven principles I discovered and how they relate to my appearance on the game show. It is my hope that you will be able to apply them to win in life and build meaningful relationships with others.

FIRST THINGS FIRST

Every day is a gift from God to you. Each new day is an opportunity to win. And today is the first day of the rest of your life! You'd be amazed at what you can accomplish if you apply these seven principles to your thought process, daily activities, and overall life.

Affirmation:

Read this affirmation aloud every day!

I will read this content with an open and willing heart. I will lead with my head, love with my heart, and keep my eyes open for every opportunity and experience. I will confront the issues that I have suppressed and ignored. I will dig deep into my conscious and subconscious thinking to evaluate where I have come from, my current situation, and where I dream my life will take me. I will find a positive message tucked between these lines. I will overcome adversity and obstacles. Regardless of ANY adversities that I may encounter, I know that I am more than a conqueror. From this day forward, my life will forever be changed.

INTRODUCTION

August 17 was like a dream. I could hardly believe that the time was right for a huge win, as each moment drew me closer to that golden moment! My trip to Las Vegas was a turning point in my life. And as you know, when most people go to Vegas, they are eager to play bingo or card games, sit at the slot machines, or roll dice. Perhaps you know someone who would do anything— including betting their rent money— to win the jackpot!

However, Vegas is much bigger than the lottery. Some go there just to have a good time— celebrate a birthday, bachelorette party, or take advantage of one of those drive-through weddings! My trip to Las Vegas had no gambling or games on the agenda, yet I knew it was the right time to win.

I traveled to Vegas with a group of friends. The invitation to join my friend's family reunion brought us all together. There were twelve of us on that trip, yet I still wondered: "Why me? Why was I hand-picked?"

I woke up the morning of June 8, bright and early, to get on the shuttle van from Las Vegas to Los Angeles, having no idea what was in store for me. I had two missions for that vacation:

escape the monotony of my everyday life and rest! I was utterly exhausted from my busy work schedule, hectic lifestyle, and "mothering," all for the sake of one day being all that I thought I needed to be. Soon, I realized that one thing was missing in my life, and it wasn't a game— I craved balance.

Never in my wildest dreams would I have imagined hearing the words, "Kanita Washington... come on down!" from show host Drew Carey. After many years of watching my mother faithfully view *The Price is Right,* I could hardly believe I was on the show. In complete shock and excitement, the hairs on the back of my neck stood up. And in this one special moment, I had the opportunity to win.

While this was my greatest opportunity to win, I had many others, as well. I attended baby showers and birthday parties where I frequently won in fun games like: "How well do you know someone," "True or False," or "Bingo." The stakes had never been higher than the opportunity to win a gift card, a small picture frame, or something I really needed. But this time was different; this was no baby shower! I was in a show where I could walk away with more than I'd ever won in my entire life!

Success, however, comes with a cost. While I only paid $30 for my transportation from Las Vegas to Hollywood, my entire trip to Vegas cost me about $600. But walking away with the huge jackpot was nothing short of a big payoff— an incredible miracle! And if you're sitting on the edge of your seat, grazing the pages of this book to read what I won, be patient— it's coming!

Although this book is about my experience, the seven principles I share throughout this book apply to winning at the *Game of Life.* The good news is, principles don't feed on luck; life is not a game of chance. Knowing the rules is half the battle; playing by them guarantees your success! Are you ready for your big win?

LAW OF FAMILIARITY: I DOUBLE DARE YOU TO MOVE

The law of familiarity is the belief that the moment you transition from what's common or customary, you'll quickly transcend into the unknown. What's in the unknown? The win! Exiting what's familiar starts in the mental space, first. Then, it converts to the environmental. We must exit right so we can enter right.

ears ago, I appeared on the *Bobby Jones Gospel* show and sang a duet entitled "Favor Ain't Fair" by Kim Stratton. I can't help but remember the song's first line: "Favor ain't fair, but it sure feels fabulous." Over time, this song has become part of me.

What is favor? Favor can be described as special treatment or a preference for someone or something. Understanding this concept going forward is essential because *favor ain't fair.* Despite any disdain shown toward you, no one is able to remove the favor that has been bestowed upon you. It's like an invisible layer of oil that shines upon your head, but only the designated persons that possess the keys to your success will recognize who you are and respond to the grace over your life.

Although we are all endowed with diverse talents, not everyone is given the same opportunities. We all have assignments in life, and this journey will feel easier for some than others. Thus, some refer to it as *luck*, some refer to it as a *blessing*, but I call it *favor*.

The thing about favor is that people don't always realize that it took you hell to get a taste of heaven. Those that witness you "tasting heaven" rarely understand "the hell" that you had to go through to get it. And at the sight of your favor, they may become envious. But we shouldn't let others' narrow-minded opinions hold us back from taking the path God has called us to. What good is it to hold your feet at the door of heaven just because someone thinks you are unworthy of his favor?

The only way for me to find bliss and peace was to step outside of my unhealthy, chaotic lifestyle. I certainly had an excursion, but the journey opened up the door to greater adventure than I ever imagined. Taking this trip went against all odds. My son, Jeremiah, was going to India for three weeks, and my daughter was going to Massanutten for our family vacation that I attended every year. To make matters worse, I was in a toxic relationship, and my partner was unwilling to let me go by myself to Vegas without him. He had serious trust issues, and this was the fire that melted our relationship. I decided to abandon the toxicity— and boy, it wasn't easy! But I thank God I did it. I didn't know it then, but stepping out was a blessing in disguise.

"Maybe I should just go to Massanutten and watch my daughter and my niece play in the pool all day and take them to each activity they desired," were my first thoughts. Then, I heard, "Kanita— GO to Vegas! Thus, going to Massanutten, Virginia, would have been direct disobedience to God.

Some family members placed me on a first-class "guilt trip"

for going to Las Vegas instead of the annual family vacation spot. All I really wanted to do was clear some "headspace" and relax. Being able to get away from it all was exciting, but it also came at a cost. I sat in the shuttle van writing a discourse that I believe I will speak on one day titled "Broken for Multiplication."

As I wrote, we departed Vegas and traveled to Hollywood. It was impossible for me to anticipate what was about to transpire. I enjoyed the sense of adventure and traveling into the unknown. As I was lost in my writing, I realized that all areas of my life— even the ones that seemed bleak and hopeless— can be employed for my good.

One of the most powerful forces that can hinder us is ourselves. Filled with shame and guilt, "Kanita, you are a failure!" played over and over in my mind. Yet, God was giving me a sign just like beams of light over broken pieces of a shattered mirror. Stepping out showed me something I would've never known; the broken pieces in my life could still shine lights of glory. After all the hell that I experienced, to even come on the trip proved that God had a master plan. So against all odds, I stayed the course, obeyed God's voice, and went.

In life, sometimes you just have to go for it! Push aside all doubt and fear and just do it! Remember, in life, we are here for a *good* time, not a *long* time, so make the best of it. So, what has been lingering in your mind to accomplish that seems so bizarre or outlandish that you have not accomplished yet? It could be something so farfetched that it causes others to really think you are crazy.

Well, here's a good place to pause and say, "Do it!" Like God's still, small voice instructed me, "Go, Kanita," I'm now saying to you, _____ (*fill your name in the blank*), to go for it! Yes, you! You have permission to live your life to the fullest!

Perhaps, you can go on a trip or find a place right at home in your little space of tranquility and simply declare: I will have balance! A newfound balance will keep you focused on what's essential in life. With balance in place, you'll be able to self-reflect and determine what's best for you so you can maintain peace and balance. Simply put, balance will cause you to pay attention to the smallest signals in your life and environment that point you in the right direction. Something as simple as a chat, a passing stranger, or a song flowing through your iTunes playlist can give you that nudge to go, stop, wait, or run for the hills!

Affirmation

Write this affirmation down and read it with conviction!

I will have balance in my life. I will take time to listen to that soft, gentle voice that cannot be ignored. I will drown out all the noise to connect to where I should be and when I should be there. I will not miss any purposeful moments because I am distracted by anyone or anything. I am focused on what is important to me and those I love. I will accomplish all of my goals on my schedule. Although this is not a peaceful world, peace will live in me because I will no longer be influenced by any negativity.

LAW OF RISK: SEIZE THE SIGNS

*The law of risk is the calculated, innate decision to no longer be
paralyzed by fear, but be arrested by faith! Faith translates to risk.
Where there is faith, there will always be a risk taken. The risk is
stepping out into the unknown to tread upon murky waters in order to
attain to a victorious win! It's time to grab ahold of your hope and
move in faith.*

s I rode in the van, lost in my thoughts, the scenery
began to change from the hills and mountains of Vegas
to the bumper-to-bumper traffic of Hollywood. My group had
planned to leave the hotel by 6:00 a.m., but if you have ever
traveled with a group, you know people are always on their own
time. It was rush hour in California, and the traffic was unbe-
lievable!

As we approached the Hollywood sign, I pulled out my
phone to snap a picture. I quickly learned that signs would be
an essential part of my trip. I'd seen Hollywood signs in movies

and TV shows, but never imagined I would see it in person. We continued our ride, and we finally arrived at the set location.

Just as we approached, I did what everyone else did— snap as many pictures as possible. I recognized the CBS sign that I had seen on TV so many times. I was there! And I visited CBS just to view *The Price is Right*— or so I thought.

Before the creation of VHS, my dad was an unofficial game show commentator. If my mom wasn't home to watch the show, she'd call him at 11:40 a.m. sharp to get the rundown on what was happening. She was a true fan, and I had one job when I got to Los Angeles— get a t-shirt for mom.

My dad would tell my mom all about the trips, cars, and prizes that the contestants were offered. Together, they would guess to see whose choice was closest, as if they were contestants on the show. This was their "daily date" that they refused to reschedule for anyone or anything. It was to the point that if my dad had to click over on the phone— someone better be dead or dying. So, I truly understood just how much getting a t-shirt meant to my mom!

Standing in line outside the CBS station, my friend and I eagerly awaited entry. Favor found me, as my name appeared on the contestant list; I was given contestant number 150! How did that happen? This experience showed me how to pay attention to the signs that push you into your favor. As we grow in faith, we learn that favor cannot always be explainable; remember— *favor ain't fair!*

What are the writings on the wall, signposts, road lights, and milestones surrounding your life this season? Are you able to be more intentional about the signs of your time and indicators for your next move?

Affirmation

Write this affirmation down and read it with conviction!

As I journey from my "when" to my "win," I will not apologize for my success in life. I am thankful and will show gratitude for all that has been afforded to me. I will be humble and stay clear of pride so that success can have a continual flow in my life. I will not be so busy that I miss the most important opportunities in my life. I am committed to paying attention to even the smallest signs.

LAW OF ISOLATION: DISPEL THE DISTRACTIONS

The law of isolation is the intentional posture of solitude and stillness. If we break down the word "isolate," it appears as "i-so-late." Say it out loud for hearing purposes! When we don't isolate ourselves, we can quickly become inundated with noise, others' issues, and external forces that we can potentially "show up late" for our time to win. Isolation is needed to listen to your inner man and the key to arriving on time.

Several things influence what we do and why we do them. And yes, personal feelings, opinions, and perceptions are important, but when it comes to principles that make you win, objectivity trumps emotions.

Objectivity is at the core of life's principles— gravity, quantum theory, and several laws of nature respond to cause and effect. For instance, it's objectively true that humans cannot survive under water regardless of how they feel about it. And although principles aren't necessarily our friends, they can be put to good use when we abide by its grounds of objectivity. The same applies to drowning out the noise.

In order to drown out the noise, you need to prioritize what makes a difference in your life. It's important to consider the things you give life to— the final decision is yours!

For me, drowning out the noises became a priority as I stepped closer to my big win! But the noises were not the same as those that radiated from Fremont Avenue's streets or the strip in Las Vegas. It wasn't even the clicking of slot machines or the shuffling of decks of cards that were on the Black Jack table. The noises I had to drown out blasted from my past and clattered all the way from the chaos I tried to escape. I tried to escape the noise of people, social media, work, children, relationships, and stress. Ultimately, I had to give life to my voice and get a chance to win by drowning the noise of others trying to influence my decisions, telling me what was and wasn't right for me. They said it wasn't the right time for my trip. Or was it?

Let's pause for a moment!

To get off the "when" and join the "winners," you must be mindful of who you have in your life and to whom you listen. Sadly, the wrong person can trigger a pattern of bad decisions that can result in life-altering casualties.

In my case, the noises in my life tried to push me off the wagon that led to beautiful moments and remarkable success. Inadvertently, I canceled my airline ticket twice as a result of doubting my trip. I began to contemplate staying behind or traveling somewhere closer, offering every excuse as to why this trip was completely bad timing.

I suspect you may be reading this and wondering: "Why stay back when you know God told you to go?" Although I acknowledged His directive, I was in a constant war with the noises that screamed, "Stay back; don't go for it!"

You see, our internal battles may cause us to miss our moments and leave us making excuses for not doing so. Let me pose this question: "Was *The Price is Right* show in Massanutten?" Definitely not! I may have one day played *The Price is Right* on the Wii gaming system, but I would not have been present on the show if I chose to go to Massanutten— that's for sure!

So, why settle for less than the best? I encourage you to follow the signs that God shows you in life, each and every day. Follow His directives because He offers direction that's void of the need for fear, thereby maximizing life-changing opportunities. Drown out the noise in your life, so you can give life to your voice!

Now, back to the story...

Once we arrived at CBS, the second type of noise I had to drown out was that of various people and the chatter of an ecstatic crowd. The space got so loud that several staff members had to consistently remind people to lower their voices.

People sang and danced in rhapsodic jubilee, all because they made it onto the show. And why not? Everyone has a reason to be excited every time favor smiles upon them! Selected individuals saw others turned away for being tardy or due to space limitations, regardless of who you were and how many tickets you preordered!

Need I remind you that favor ain't fair? While many didn't receive the opportunity, God's favor enabled me to have a place on the show. Once again, favor ain't fair!

As if being on the show wasn't enough, we were handed an opportunity to meet and impress the producer. At that point, my heart skipped a beat and my palms began to sweat profusely; in fact, nervousness hardly defines all that was happening to me!

Beyond the noise in the room, there was more going on in

my head. In that moment, I realized how much I needed a control-zone—a quiet headspace—in order to get my head over the sand and face the game. Of course, it may seem like I'm being too deep, but how many opportunities have we missed by not involving the Holy Spirit— even in the smallest decisions of our lives?

When was the last time you were distracted by the noise around and inside you? How many opportunities have you missed because you did not get into a still, quiet place to effectively hear God's voice? Every winner understands how to tune out the noise, zoom out of the chaos, and attune their ears to God's still, small voice.

The next page has been intentionally left blank so you can reflect and write down those missed opportunities.

———

Reflect on some of the opportunities you felt you may have missed due to allowing the noise to overpower God's still, soft voice.

_____

_____

_____

_____

_____

_____

_____

_____

_____

_____

_____

_____

_____

_____

_____

_____

_____

_____

_____

_____

_____

_____

_____

_____

_____

_____

_____

As I waited to meet with the producer, I was completely quiet. I had to drown out the noise of the laughter and singing, to come up with an idea that would impress the producer. I was digging in the dirt to find my diamond.

Earlier, I came to the show just to sit in the audience, and when I realized that I could be a contestant, it was on! Playtime was over! This was not a game! All I could think about was what would impress the producer? I needed something that would hit the bull's eye! I imagined what I could say that would cause me to stand out from amongst the other 300 people who came to spin the big wheel.

In the stillness, springs of ideas began to surge. I thought that perhaps I should sing my name, but then I mentally inflected, "Kanita, this is not American Idol. Get a grip!" Boy, I was hungry for a win and ready to walk onto the show set wearing my"girl on fire" dress.

Now, don't get me wrong, I had lots of fun! I took a few selfies and pictures, but my prime objective was to emerge as a contestant. I thought long and hard! Then I discovered an effective strategy that would direct my arrow into the heart of the producer.

When it was my group's turn to be assessed, I was the first in line, but this was not the typical queue. The producer looked straight in my eye, and his voice flooded the room, "What is your name, and where are you from?" I replied, "I'm Kanita Washington from D.C. and I'm coming to see DC— Drew Carey, baby"! I was so excited! And little did I know, it was in that moment that I hit the bull's eye!

Affirmation

Write this affirmation down and read it with conviction!

I will arrive at my life's destination on time. I will drown out every noise and distraction that could disrupt my destiny or delay my progress. I will tune out the chatter of doubt and negativity while I tune into the frequency of confidence and optimism. My ideas and goals will hit the bull's eye. I will not miss the mark or my target.

LAW OF DETERMINATION: SNATCH YOUR FOCUS

The law of determination is the commitment to allow your conscious mind the ability to impress the idea of determination upon your subconscious mind, birthing the "winner's mentality." Once the "winner's mentality" is conceived in the mind, it will manifest in our reality. But first, there has to be a mental transaction of determination before it can translate into the natural realm.

"Come on down!" the anchor blared. Now, even when I heard him call my name and saw the poster board with my name on it, somehow my knees locked in their socket and I could not move due to shock! I could not believe that I made it! I won!

One thing's for sure— I was completely astonished! Perhaps you may not be able to fully relate to my amazement, but one thing is certain, there are times in life when it seems like the spotlight is suddenly beaming upon you. And in that moment you may realize, all eyes are on you! You are in the spotlight!

So, are you ready to step out of the shadows into the spotlight? Are you prepared to take in the shocking aura of glory? Are you ready to win? If so, let's make this declaration together.

I declare that everything in my life will be aligned in my favor. God is about to announce my name. I will be ready to step into my destiny, and I will be ready to be showcased. What I prayed for in the dark will manifest itself in the light! There are blessings with my name on them! I must prepare myself to receive every good gift that is on the hunt for me!

If you believe and receive what you declared, then sign your name on the dotted line: _____

Every blessing God releases moves towards its recipients like a guided missile. This is why I believe that some blessings in life are tailored for you with your name on it. However, there are others that aren't just for you! I've seen doors of blessings that are wide enough to bless its recipient and others years down the line!

Remember, a good man leaves an inheritance for his children's children. Therefore, we must understand the difference between what God gives each of us for ourselves and what God has given to us to share with others. God's blessing is not to be shared with everybody, so we must choose carefully. Here's a pearl of profound wisdom: Jesus said, "...do not throw your pearls before pigs, lest they trample them underfoot and turn to attack you." With this insight, it's essential that we don't throw away our valuables to those who aren't capable of or positioned to receive them.

You were handpicked to receive a blessing and to be a blessing. So, consider those who you desire to be a blessing to. Ensure that you select wisely. Make a commitment to bless two people when your blessing comes in! I did, and I have reaped the benefits of what I sowed into their lives. Therefore, I am leading by example and wouldn't ask you to do anything that I have not also personally done.

So, which names will you fill in below?

_____   _____

Blessing Recipient #1   **Blessing Recipient #2**

When your blessings come, remember to be cautious of pride. You did not make it to the top of the mountain so that people can see you and recognize you! While I encourage you to enjoy your "heaven," be mindful of the "hell" you had to go through. Remember that not everyone survived the same process that refined you.

Don't get things twisted; it takes a good attitude to manage success. Making it to the top for the wrong reasons— to be seen or for acclamation— has never benefited anyone. It takes hard work and grit to get to the top, but it takes character to stay there. We often find people whose character doesn't sustain them when they reach what we call the mountain top. So, step out of those grim statistics and be different. Pride will cause you to lose everything— remain humble.

One of my most humbling experiences happened as I went to sign the paperwork after winning the game show. I took out my identification, but realized that I left my wallet and purse in the chair. While completing the paperwork, someone stole my wallet. I had just won the showcase, but an embarrassing situation like a missing wallet began a tug-of-war for my joy. So, I had to fight to keep my eyes on the big picture! I refused to allow someone who stole my wallet to also snatch my joy.

But here's the blessing! I had $150 in my wallet— does that number ring a bell? (I was the 150th contestant!) God was revealing to me in that moment that He can take what seemed to be a curse and bless me so much that even what was lost or taken will not compare to the blessings that will eventually overtake me!

So, I canceled most of my credit cards, but I did leave one other card in my hotel room. I could have focused on the fact that someone dared to steal from me. It could have been a random stranger or even someone who I was vacationing with. Rather than focus on the downside of the situation, I focused my attention on the joy.

They say you can't have rainbows without rain. And that's exactly what I was facing! I overcame pride in a battle of wills to force me to concentrate on myself and not recognize that I was recently blessed beyond measure.

In the midst of the most rewarding time of your life, difficulty and disappointment may still be a part of the story. However, it is in those difficult moments that we have to focus on the important things.

So, how does this work? Well, it's almost like attempting to take a picture from a distance. You have to zoom in on what you want to capture. Many things aren't appealing on a micro level. Imagine viewing a painting with a microscope— from an ant's view or at a micro-distance— how would you possibly be able to appreciate such a work of art? How can you connect the dots in your life and appreciate its beauty when you zoom in on the negative dimensions of your experience?

Oftentimes, our pride brings us to a place of depression and anxiety when we take a picture of our lives from a zoomed-in camera. And when we try to zoom in, the question is, what are we focusing on? Are we looking at the opportunity in the challenge or the problem in the potential? Ignoring other things around, as we focus on what we believe is most significant at a particular moment, can be a blessing or a bane.

I refused to allow pride to adjust my lens for me. I zoomed in on the blessings, and I was too engrossed to even think, blame, or even wonder why that happened. I'm fully convinced that I was being tested! And as long as I stayed grateful for what I had, I paralyzed the pride in my mind that wanted me to focus on what seemed to have been lost.

Affirmation

Write this affirmation down and read it with conviction!

I am postured to be ready and to receive every blessing designed for me. I am thankful and humbled by this life exploration. I am wiser because of yesterday, blessed to experience today, and anticipate the journey of tomorrow. I will not be distracted by anything that attempts to compete with my blessing. I will zoom in and focus on what is important to me. I will focus on the positive aspects of life and emphasize my mental welfare and personal peace. I will not let the acts of others dictate my actions or words. I am happy because I choose to be!

LAW OF RELEASE: RELEASE THE WEIGHT OF YOUR WAIT

The law of release is the liberation from the heavy weight of waiting for the ultimate win. Subconsciously, we often hold onto doubt, which becomes a hinderance because it takes so long to win. But when we release those weights, it not only lightens the load, but frees you mentally from the burden of the wait.

$\mathcal{T}$ime is the currency of life. And life often forces us into the waiting game where we strive to keep our heads above the water, as we swim across the ocean of countless moments of doubt and anxiety, before we reach the shores of what we call success.

I was thrust into the waiting game right after August 17, 2015. I had to wait until the viewing of the show, which was scheduled for November 20, 2015 in order to hear the big news and collect my winnings. Legally, I could not tell anyone anything!

And guess what, after August 17, all hell broke loose! This bill was due and that bill was due! There was tension in my relationship and stress at my job. It seemed as if everything that could go wrong did. I kept constantly reminding myself, "It's not what happens to you; it's how you respond to it that shows true character… and, this too, shall pass!"

Then the big day arrived! I didn't win any cash. But guess what, the experience and winnings up until November 20 were more than rewarding! And perhaps you're feeling sorry for me. Well, don't miss the blessings in disguise!

First, it's not always a good thing to win monetarily. Sometimes it's better to walk away with something tangible. Besides, I was glad I didn't have to face what life would be like for me if I won lots of money and later lost it because of mismanagement. That's a storyline we hear all too often.

Being a participant on the show came with a contract, and to receive the prizes came with strict stipulations. And like most contracts between two parties, it is advised that you thoroughly read the small print. The small print generally tells you the intricate details that will totally forfeit a contract if you don't adhere to all the terms. The contract also warns that contestants cannot disclose to anyone their winnings because the show would like to keep their ratings up, just as much as the contestants would like to keep their prizes and winnings!

So, the clock ticked… tick-tock… tick tock! It seemed as if November would never get here! All I knew was that I was patiently waiting and a little less excited about having to pay taxes on my prizes before ever receiving them. I kept wondering, "Where the heck is my stuff?"

This is one of those difficult lessons we regularly have to re-learn in life: timing is everything, so be patient. If something is truly destined for you, believe and have faith that you will receive it. Although things may not happen when you want them to, just have faith that everything happens for a reason.

You should also assess how you are playing the waiting game to examine if you're winning at it. You'll know how you're handling your waiting season by asking yourself these questions: What am I doing in the process? Am I angry, full of doubt, stressed out?

The truth is, hope deferred makes the heart sick. But that's the big test— the heart-test! So, try to release negative weight and watch everything God has for you unfold unto you. You will see that all of your blessings were right on time. Trust the process; not one blessing will be delayed.

What are some things you are currently waiting for in your life?

_____

_____

_____

Here is my prayer for whatever you are waiting on. Read this aloud, as we come into agreement together before the Lord.

Father God, I stand in agreement that every promise You have given me according to Your will shall come to pass. Father, overtake me with your love and your presence. I am so grateful for each blessing You have afforded to me already. You have already blessed me beyond measure, and even if You choose not to do the thing I've prayed to You about, I will humbly receive Your very best for me! I ask that You would continue to give me the strategy I need to receive every promise spoken by You. Lord, show me the route I must go to receive Your abundant blessings and not await what some would call a "magical experience." I pray for strategy now! Every promise comes with instructions! So, I pray that the instructions you give me will be realized and obeyed, that they may enter into every fruitful place for my family and generations to come.
In Jesus Name, Amen.

Affirmation

Write this affirmation down and read it with conviction!

I am becoming more patient, knowing that I take one step closer to becoming and owning everything I want every day. I will show grace and patience in the face of trials and tribulations. I will trust the order of God and the Universe and accept that my time is coming. I will be as patient with others as I would like them to be with me. I am certain the outcome will be for my highest benefit; so, I will wait without anxiety.

LAW OF SILENCE: QUIET YOUR QUILL

The law of silence is the protection from premature exposure. When news breaks before its time, it can cause much turmoil in the world. You must operate in wisdom when you're on the verge of a win, because telling the wrong sources can poison the outcome. Remember, not everyone will celebrate your victories or wins. Be calculated and wise. Operate in silence and allow the results to reveal itself in time.

---

*L*ife is a weave of mystery for only the skillful and wise to unravel. Sometimes, we may succeed at life's activities with a top-notch skill to match its various highs and lows. Or, we might miss the chance and let the opportunity fall through when we're untrained. As we hit the road of growth, we're pulled to rub shoulders with new experiences and novel exercises that could cause some panic if we ever let them go down the drain.

While testing the ground, we may level up to phases and attain heights that confront us with failed trials and futile tests, falling flat on our faces. In such times, we can be tempted to pick ourselves up as we shove in defeat or pretend that nothing happened, never uttering a single word of it to others!

Many can live and die with a horrible secret. But what about keeping good news a secret? Think about it. What if you received a well-deserved promotion or an expected baby just arrived and you are asked to keep silent about it?

It was once stated that the essence of our emotions—sadness or joy, happiness or sorrow, grief or grit—is to share with people who can receive, understand, and empathize with us. How do you tuck in the tail of your much awaited testimony amid the reality of it?

I think we've all been privy to a juicy secret that felt as if it would just burst out of you! That's how I felt in my case. I had just competed and won on one of my favorite game shows. *Talk about a conversation starter!* What happened to me could've scored hundreds of discussion points and gathered many people my way! But, I had to keep my experience a secret. I had to be obedient, and therefore, seal my lips. I decided that I would not disclose this information to anyone I did not trust. The people that went with me knew and everyone else would discover by watching CBS when the show would air. I chewed on this secret the entire ride home. Undeniably, the van was hyped because most of us realized this was a blessing.

Unfortunately, not everyone was thrilled about my success on the show. I heard murmurs of "How did she even get on the show? She only came to *our* family reunion as a guest!" Previously, I had the impression that this experience would bond friends into family, even though I was the friend of the family. I hoped we would all hit on something even deeper at the end of the event. Everyone could come on stage because it was not just my moment; it was everyone in the family's moment. Surprisingly, I was thrown off the cliff after a closer glimpse at the heart of those that surrounded me!

The entire episode justified the fact that not everyone will revel in your success. And some folks are outrageously bold to run down your win right in your face! Ever heard of the expression: "Don't talk with your mouth full?" I believe its meaning and significance have outgrown its designated dining table usage. And here's how!

In life's broad table, you're served with various nutrients of success, favor, and breakthrough. And as you fulfill your destiny, sometimes you have to hush up, be still, and keep a secret! Are you getting my drift yet? I firmly believe that if you mishandle even the information of a promise or manipulate the commitment of your integrity, you may jeopardize the reward. Don't let your mouth forfeit your reward!

Are you concerned that you might be sharing too much information? What promise has God given you that you know you have to wait patiently for? This gift is perhaps not meant to be shared with everyone, or with anyone, for that matter. You are guarding the future that belongs to you.

It is true that life springs from the heart. So, imagine when you bear all your heart out to others. You may be placing your life's map in their hands. Oftentimes, it may be wiser to get counsel concerning an issue, but never at the expense of your destiny. Putting your future out to the world could pose the threat of negative commentaries, disbelief and discouragement, disapproval, or even revolt!

A familiar story of young Caleb McCafee, in his book, *Turning Your Dreams into Reality*, rings a bell. McCafee innocently mentioned to his uncle that he was going to be a successful entrepreneur in the future. His uncle dissuaded him from the idea because there was no entrepreneur in their bloodline who had ever made it big! As McCafee stubbornly forged on to make his inward dreams come true, he resolved that the best way to show people that you're going to do something is to do it!

As you receive all that God places in your heart, embrace

and accept it. Take this next page to write down your vision and reinforce your dreams.

Reflect and Write

Vision#1:

_____

_____

_____

_____

Vision #2:

_____

_____

_____

_____

Remember!

Some people will measure down your success as soon as you have it! You may sink into shame from nasty comments on social media or get backlashed. So, here's what you have to know: it's normal to experience this on the terrain of achievement! Don't get caught up in a web of negative emotions or attitudes of people that refuse to celebrate you!

Affirmation

Write this affirmation down and read it with conviction!

I am so appreciative of my blessings. I am thankful for the opportunity to reveal who I have the potential to become. I will learn to move on in silence and let my actions and behavior speak louder than my words. I will not allow family, friends, enemies, or even my own doubt prevent me from living in my glory and becoming all that I am destined to be. I will not be swayed by the wrong actions or swirled by the bitter words from my enemies and those posing as friends and family. I am not all that I can be yet, but I have certainly progressed from who I was. I am on my way to being the best version of myself. And that, in itself, is enough for me. I do not strive to please others at the cost of my own happiness. I will move in my own time, in my own way, and at my own pace.

LAW OF HUMILITY: ADJUST YOUR PERSPECTIVE

The law of humility is the posture of lowliness. *No matter where you go, let humility be your guide. Any time you walk in pride, you expose yourself to failure. You cannot afford to fail!*

*L*ike watching a shooting star nosedive into the sky, some memories leave us in awe! The second the show aired on TV, I could hardly believe it was real. My excitement and emotions were extreme! They exuded beyond my control! And at this juncture, I paused to give God all of the glory and credit!

So, this leads me to challenge you— whether you are awaiting a blessing or just received one, know that you have to praise God on purpose! Deliberately pause everything else to show Him your sincere gratitude; that is not a game!

As we endure life, many troubles may challenge us, but let's not forget what God says about that! Romans 8:28 reveals that: "...all things work together for good to them that love God, to them who are the called according to his purpose." We have an advantage because God created each person for a purpose. And so, we need to believe that the circumstances in our lives are working together to form a version of us that is not just the best, but also perfect!

So, as you complete the reading of this book, I am hopeful that it marks the beginning of a new life and new perspective for you. I encourage you to get a notebook, pen, or your computer and write every day! Write about what you've learned. Write on your outlook about a situation you're passing through. Be intentional with your day and schedule time to journal your experiences, stories, hopes, desires, and all that you are grateful for!

It's time! The game is on, and here's the real game changer to get you to your win— write!

The things I am grateful for are:

_____

_____

_____

_____

_____

Daily Prayer

God, I take this moment to thank You for all of Your blessings. Your blessings are absolutely immeasurable so that I cannot even describe or thank You enough for them all! Father, I pray now that You will bless each reader in an even greater way, and exceed their expectations. Show Yourself strong in their lives and let them always remember to pause and give You all the praise. Amen.

Take it from me...

When you hear God's voice say, "GO," it's time to GO!
Some people won't understand your move, nor why you're going!
Some won't celebrate you!
Some people will steal— but whoa— you touched the Big Wheel!
Some will judge your winnings as if it should be theirs!
But the big question is: Can you stand to be blessed?
That's the real test!

COME ON DOWN!
YOU'RE THE NEXT CONTESTANT ON
THE PRICE IS RIGHT!

ACKNOWLEDGMENTS

Several people have helped me to complete this book. Without their love and support, I would not have been able to do it.

I would first like to thank my Lord and Savior, Jesus Christ. Without Him, none of these experiences would be possible.

A special thank you to my parents— Mr. & Mrs. Charles and Myra Washington— your love has inspired me to always push forward!

To my children Jeremiah, Kovenant, and my God-sent Goddaughter Quiandria (also known as KeKe), you are my greatest blessings! I love each one of you!

ABOUT THE AUTHOR

Prophetess Kanita L. Washington is an internationally-renowned prophet, preacher, motivational and conference speaker who demonstrates the undeniable power and discernment of the Holy Spirit through the dynamic life shifting prophetic mantle on her life.

Throughout the years and through encounters, The Lord imparted His love, power, supernatural wisdom and compassion into her life, giving her a healing voice to the hurting, wounded, broken, and tormented. Truly, she has a ministry for the hurting.

God has launched her to minister in various churches and international platforms, prophetically, as well as in song all over the world; she is called to the nations.

Her dynamic sound of prophetic worship has such a profound impact on others that people have testified that they were healed and delivered under the sound of her voice— to the Glory of God!

Prophetess Kanita fervently yearns to serve the Lord and His people by equipping the Body of Christ through a prophetic message. Her talents are multidimensional, so much so, that she released her first book in 2016 entitled "Prophetic Triumphs: Handling Life's Most Challenging Transitions," and anticipates the release of her newest books. In May 2019, she released her first single, "Blessings, Blessings." She's also an accomplished playwright who desires to minister in the field of dramatic arts, worldwide.

She currently attends Oracle of God's Temple in Columbia, Maryland, where Chief Servant James Ephraim is the pastor. She also holds a Master's degree in Health and Human Service, which was obtained at Coppin State University, and is pursuing her Doctoral degree in Leadership and Organization.